PRAISE FOR

The New Black Woman

"*The New Black Woman* is so important for Black Women today. I love this book because it gives Black women permission and tools to learn how to take better care of themselves, particularly in a world that discourages them from doing so. Marita Golden's work is refreshing and enlightening, as it encourages more Black women to deeply know their worth and understand what self-care practices can look like. I'm so happy for more women to have this knowledge and these strategies."

—**Dr. Amber Thornton,** clinical psychologist specializing in motherhood mental health

"*The New Black Woman* isn't one of those books you read, put on a shelf, and forget about—you can't. At least you shouldn't, because if you do, you are missing the point. This is one of those books you read and re-read, letting the words slip, sit, and settle into the too-long-neglected and dark corners of your soul. This is one of those books you read every day, for thirty days, allowing the words to silently work their magic, simultaneously soothing your spirit and stirring you into self-honoring actions. This is one of those books that, in its brilliance and brevity, causes a beautiful and inevitable internal, then external shift in your beingness. This is one book that speaks truth to the power of your own self-care, self-love, self-worth, self-compassion, self-esteem, self-support, self-discovery, self-indulgence, self-preservation, self-confidence, and self-honor. This is one book you can't forget because it guides you to who you really are. It will transform your emotional life, if you will just open up all of your many selves to the goodness and selfless wisdom that is Marita Golden."

—**Michelle Petties,** food story coach and author of *Leaving Large: The Stories of a Food Addict*

"Marita Golden has done it again! With grace, wisdom and fortitude, she's written another powerful love letter to Black women. *The New Black Woman* is a how-to guide on extracting the essentials for fulfillment, first and foremost, from within. Through the pages of this new work, she issues a call to arms, entreating Black women not to be strong and relentless (as we are every day), but to be honest and introspective. That is the first step to radical resilience and tapping into our physical, mental and spiritual health to soar. This book, like so many of Marita's expositions, takes us on a journey of truth and discovery. It is an easy read that travels full circle and ends up in a new place of awareness and connectedness. In the end, she challenges us to be who we are and, in so doing, that person we are destined to become."

—**Gwen McKinney,** creator of *Unerased | Black Women Speak*

PRAISE FOR
Marita Golden's
Other Works

THE STRONG BLACK WOMAN

"If ever there was a book for these times, for Black women, for Black people and for all people of all races and genders, *The Strong Black Woman* is it. Both painful and hopeful, instructive over that which could be, and all too often is, destructive, Marita Golden provides, in her words, 'a healing balm' even for those who believe they have no need. Through her own often-painful history and revealing glimpses of other women who have had to work through pain many would find unimaginable, Golden's journey is along a road that, in the end, is filled with trees bearing fruit of a very special life and lives, thankfully shared by one of our most powerful writers."

—**Charlayne Hunter-Gault**, American civil rights activist, journalist, and former foreign correspondent for NPR, CNN, and PBS

"Necessary and relevant, *The Strong Black Woman* shows the time is now to let go of what no longer serves you. Love—whether it is loving others or yourself—is the most important thing. It is a doorway for compassion, kindness, gratitude, and well-being. Marita Golden's moving personal narrative invites you to step through a new door, to be with yourself, and ultimately, to love yourself in only the way you know how."

—**Bridgitte Jackson-Buckley**, blogger, interviewer, memoirist, and author of *The Gift of Crisis*

"Part poetic meditation, part research-driven journalism, Marita Golden's *The Strong Black Woman* examines the issues surrounding Black women's health and delves into the history of oppression that continues to endanger Black women today. Golden is adept in her prose and delivers a bold, honest, unflinching gaze at the myriad issues impacting Black women. She emboldens her readers to become New Age Strong Black Women who prevail over their history and rise from the ashes of the past with a brave understanding of what it means to be Black and female in the world today. These essays are creative, inventive, and necessary."

—**M.J. Fievre**, educator, editor, playwright, and author of the *Badass Black Girl* series

"Marita Golden's *The Strong Black Woman* busts the myth that Black women are fierce and resilient by letting the reader in under the mask that proclaims 'Black don't crack.' Golden shows all the cracks and fissures in a clear, ringing voice that examines a multitude of issues facing Black women today. In revealing what's really under the mask of strength Black women wear, Golden exposes the vulnerability of Black women, but also manages to forge a new vision of Black femininity that is stronger and more resilient than anyone has imagined. *The Strong Black Woman* is important to consider when reflecting on the #MeToo era and should be required reading for anyone who considers herself to be a feminist. It illuminates the present while scouring the past, and points to a future where Black women can be vibrant, healthy, and equally considered members of society."

—**Karen Arrington**, coach, mentor, philanthropist, and author of NAACP Image Award–winning *Your Next Level Life*

"In *The Strong Black Woman*, Marita shares her own joys and pains and what has made her the literary force we know. Through the art of storytelling and the wisdom garnered through her research we are able to experience the truth, that the strong Black woman is not just a troupe that is the reflection of our trauma but is the truth of our brilliance. The book does what Marita has always done, use story to offer Black women a reflection of our lives and a way to grow. *Strong Black Woman* is as much an act of literary activism as every effort that Marita Golden puts forth. Bravo for writing a book that will long benefit us all."

—**Zelda Lockhart**, author of the novel *Fifth Born*

"*The Strong Black Woman* shatters the myth and the burden that too many of us have carried for too long while holding up villages and fighting for justice. By the end of the first chapter, I was nearly in tears. I was ready to send the book to my mother, sisters, cousins, nieces, and best friends. *The Strong Black Woman* gives us explanations for the pain and histories that our mothers couldn't or wouldn't tell us, a book that is required reading for every person—Black, White, man, woman, and child—who wants to remain healthy and survive in a world that wants otherwise."

—**DeNeen L. Brown**, award-winning writer for the *Washington Post* and producer of the documentary *Tulsa the Fire and the Forgotten*

SAVING OUR SONS

"It is always heartening to see women step up to the writer's table. When the results are as adroit and affecting as Marita Golden's work, it is more than satisfying; it is a cause for celebration."

—**Toni Morrison**, Nobel Laureate

"Marita Golden has captured the special pain that shadows the joy of Black parenthood in these turbulent times. Elegantly written, this book is a breakthrough."

—*Chicago Tribune*

"A wonderful storyteller, an uncompromising mind, Marita Golden explores the African–American experience in a completely original way."

—*Newsweek*

"In this book, Marita reminds us why every Black parent should be vigilant and intentional in considering how to steer young Black boys—and girls as well—through the precarious passage to adulthood.

Saving Our Sons is disturbingly relevant in this, the twenty-first century. It's a compelling read."

—**Nathan McCall**, author of *Makes Me Wanna Holler: A Young Black Man in America*

"Marita Golden's *Saving Our Sons* was revelatory when first published and remains so today. *Saving Our Sons* is a superb mother's, artist's, teacher's, and community activist's love story of her son and by extension, all Black sons. This is a book that provides life lessons for our daughters too. *Saving Our Sons* is critical as a guide, motivator, love note, and an avenue into lifesaving discussions of the heart for all Black children."

—**Haki R. Madhubuti,** founder of Third World Press and author of *Black Men: Obsolete, Single, Dangerous* (1991) and *Taught By Women: Poems As Resistance Language, New and Selected* (2020)

The New Black Woman

BOOKS BY
Marita Golden

The New
Black
Woman

LOVES HERSELF,

HAS BOUNDARIES, AND

HEALS EVERY DAY

MARITA GOLDEN

mango
PUBLISHING
CORAL GABLES

For permission requests, please contact the publisher at:
Mango Publishing Group
2850 S Douglas Road, 2nd Floor
Coral Gables, FL 33134 USA
info@mango.bz

For special orders, quantity sales, course adoptions and corporate sales, please email the publisher at sales@mango.bz. For trade and wholesale sales, please contact Ingram Publisher Services at customer.service@ingramcontent.com or +1.800.509.4887.

The New Black Woman: Loves Herself, Has Boundaries, and Heals Every Day

Library of Congress Cataloging-in-Publication number: 2023930420
ISBN: (pb) 978-1-6848w1-222-6 (hc) 978-1-68481-285-1
(e) 978-1-68481-223-3
BISAC category code SOC001000, SOCIAL SCIENCE / Ethnic Studies / American / African American & Black Studies

Contents

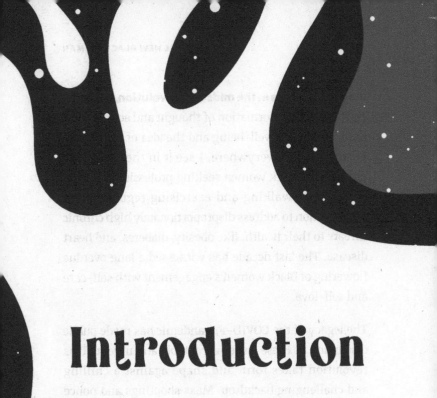

Introduction

Black women are in the midst of a revolution, a seismic shift, a radical reformation of thought and action about their health and well-being and the idea of being well. I see the signs everywhere. I see it in the increasing numbers of Black women seeking professional mental health care, walking and exercising regularly, and taking action to address disproportionately high chronic threats to their health, like obesity, diabetes, and heart disease. The last decade has witnessed a long overdue flowering of Black women's engagement with self-care and self-love.

The legacy of the COVID-19 pandemic has made public discussion of these issues acceptable and urgent. This revolution takes form and shape against a chilling and challenging backdrop. Mass shootings and police violence are now normalized; our healthcare system is broken even as more people gain coverage. Income inequality increases annually. We are grappling with the impact of social media on our psyches and our lives. This revolution is happening even as too many, including myself, feel like our country is experiencing a psychotic break.

And so, health physical and mental, the strength and resilience of our souls and spirits are subjects that we all own, and that must concern us all. This revolution is creating a new type of Black woman. I call her the New Black Woman. She is twenty-three, forty-five, and seventy. And she is the inheritor of a decade or more of activism, scholarship, research, community, and public discourse about the challenges Black women face in maintaining health and vibrant spirits.

Today's New Black Woman listened when Michelle Obama initiated a national discussion about mental health. She has seen the real-life positive effect of meeting head-on health and mental health challenges, leading the way to healing and bringing friends and family along with her. Today's New Black Woman is pressing to change the American medical system's generations-old racism whether the issue is Black maternal care or the need to simply hear Black women's testimony about their health. She is not fearful. She is in charge.

The health statistics that seem to doom Black women to early death spur today's New Black Woman to discuss life, living, and dying, with family and friends easily and openly. Today's New Black Woman takes time and makes time for herself without apology or the need to explain or seek permission.

This book is a meditation on the practices and beliefs about mental and physical health as well as spiritual well-being that have been the foundation of my life for most of my life. This is a book about how each day I learn anew how to honor myself.

I honor myself. Honor yourself. That is a radical idea in the Black community. Even against the backdrop of the sexual revolution, feminism, a Black First Lady, a Black female vice president, Black female astronauts, and surgeons, the idea that Black women have the right and the duty to honor themselves remains incomprehensible to many men and women in our families.

The three pillars of health for me are a deep and enduring relationship with myself and my spirit, my "inner Marita," being willing to say yes to what affirms and celebrates me and no to what can harm me, and treating my body with love, respect, and constant care. So many readers asked me, after the publication of *The Strong Black Woman*, to write more about my personal practices. *The New Black Woman* is my response and my gift to those readers and to you.

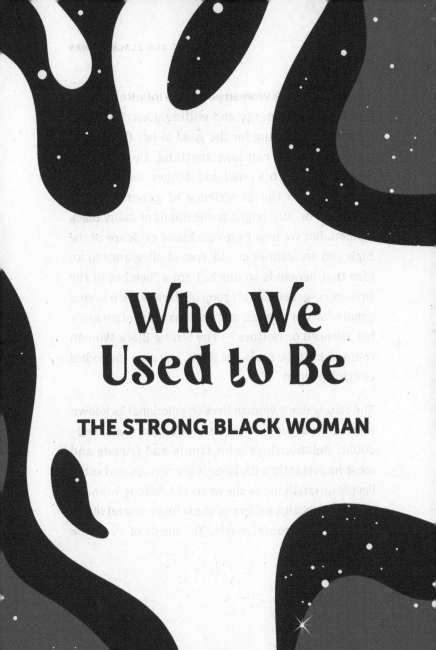

Who We Used to Be

THE STRONG BLACK WOMAN

The Strong Black Woman possesses infinite physical and emotional energy and willingly sacrifices her personal well-being for the good of her family and community. She can take anything. Do anything. She is a rock. This cruel and dangerous belief, an adaptation to the experience of generations of enslavement, still reigns in the minds of many Black women. But we now have conclusive evidence of the high and sometimes deadly cost of allegiance to an idea that demands so much. I am a member of the first cross-generational group of Black women saying aloud what our mothers and grandmothers often knew but silenced or censored—The Strong Black Woman complex kills the souls, the spirit, and even the bodies of Black women.

The Strong Black Woman lives on emotional lockdown muting the expression of fear, uncertainty, and self-doubt. Relationships with family and friends and most importantly with herself are corrupt and often deeply unsatisfying as she wears the "strong woman" mask. Her health suffers as she refuses to tend to her physical and mental needs. The needs of everyone else come first.

"Black women are the most neglected women in America. They are neglected by their families. And they neglect themselves."

–Audrey Chapman,
FAMILY THERAPIST

PART I

Embracing Silence as Self-Care

"It's never been safe for Black women to show their true emotions. Often on their jobs, they feel that they may be penalized by Whites and that what they say could negatively impact other Black people. And even at home, they may not feel free to express what they feel. So Black women have to learn how to own their emotions. In the search for contentment, I ask my clients where they feel safe. Where do they feel comfortable? *You* should be your happy place.

Can you be comfortable in your body and your mind? *You* should be your safe space. Your body goes with you wherever you go so you should be in your safe space wherever you are. Fill your life with what I call 'pockets of joy.' What can you do for yourself for ten minutes that makes you feel good? Drink a cup of tea, slowly and savor its flavors, read a few pages of a book. Start with ten minutes and build up to longer periods of 'Happy Place Time.'"

–Dr. Raquel Martin,
CLINICAL PSYCHOLOGIST

I begin this book by writing about silence because I believe reconciliation with the beauty and power of our souls is the foundation for all the good we do in our lives and the world. Silence as we meditate. Silence as we pray. Silence during long walks. Silence while sitting still. Silence just because. In silence, we connect with our intuition, our inner wisdom, and the expansiveness of our hearts. And when we do that, we can set boundaries and we can care for our bodies and minds with compassion and dedication.

I found myself in silence. Silence, the very idea of which provokes fear and wonder. Silence is both a mystery and an answer. There is the silence of our mother's womb. There is the silence we enter at death. Silence is a beginning and an end. I have found myself by entering silence through meditation and practicing intentional, intended hours, and days of quiet and stillness. I have created a replenishing, necessary space in my life. Silence is a door that I never fully close, that I never lock, a room I enter easily and often.

I love being a silent Black woman.

In silence, I have met my*self*. That seed of my soul blossoms outside the shadow of family, friends, enemies, White folks, fear, racism, the Race, and the demons of should, could, and would. This self, this spirit, this autonomous yet integral *me*, is the most important part of my *self*. This is a self that many of us never meet.

Black women are conditioned, raised, and told to be outer-directed, to accomplish, to do, for themselves, and the greater good of our people. We carry ourselves, our families, and the larger racial family on our shoulders as we cross the finish line. The forty-plus years during which I have developed a vibrant, even passionate, practice of silence and in which I have allowed myself to hear and to feel have been enormously creative and productive. Years during which I integrated the precious inner self into my outer self. The inner self no one sees but that is part of my beating heart allows me to shape my life rather than receive it like a blueprint from others. Silence has been a cradle of stillness, an incubator for the language I need to live a life of my choosing, and a place where I fell in love with my soul and my body.

I began practicing meditation in my early twenties, initially becoming a practitioner and devotee of Transcendental Meditation, developed by the Indian spiritual figure Maharishi Mahesh Yogi. The practice involves the use of a private mantra and is practiced for twenty minutes twice a day while sitting comfortably with one's eyes closed. I regularly experienced relaxation, and inner calm and began to try to weave those emotions more frequently into the fabric of my life as I lived it day-to-day in real-time. I felt more creative and efficient and slept better.

As my interest in various forms of meditation grew, I began reading more about the work of the Vietnamese Buddhist Monk Thich Nhất Hanh and his mindfulness meditation practices, which focused on becoming aware of your breath and living in the present moment. Practicing meditation and exploring this new spiritual world increased my longing for ways that I could actively counter the anxiety and obsessive thinking about the past, my mistakes, and the future that so often derailed contentment. Until I began this continuing journey, I had no concept of joy or peace, or contentment that was not connected to achievement or material gain. I was a fiction writer who persistently used my imagination yet could not have imagined that

I would discover my life as inherently a repository of the miraculous, the seat of bountiful spiritual blessings that I could reveal easily and naturally.

Like many of us, I have had a complicated relationship with the idea of silence. The idea of *being* silent is distinctly different from wanting the environment around us to *be* silent. Many of us are frightened by silence for many reasons. We don't know ourselves and fear that silence will incite recurring fearful thoughts we have yet to master. We live in a society that discourages silence and alone time. We have to be busy, working, or accomplishing something and we see being silent as unproductive and a waste of time. We are suspicious of people who want to be alone and don't always need to be out with the crowd. Practicing meditation chipped away at any residual negative feelings I had about silence because in meditation, that's what I was, *silent.*

The idea of practicing longer periods of silence was inspired by a boyfriend whom I was living with. Our relationship was stormy. It was the kind of relationship in which I think we both felt trapped rather than freed by our feelings for each other. Despite loving this man, I never felt that I knew him, a red flag I was blind to for too long. We lived together and there were days when he would practice silence in the apartment with me yet apart, entering a world where he sought, I think, healing and replenishment. I meditated. He practiced periods of silence. None of that saved our relationship.

Several years later, content and married to another man, I had become a published author of several books. There was the mysterious yet fulfilling world in which I created my books. Then there was the other world of selling my books, praying for good reviews of my books, and trying to slay the green-eyed monster of jealousy if a fellow writer experienced recognition, material success, awards, and great reviews that exceeded my experience. After an awful review of one of my books in my hometown newspaper, the *Washington Post*, I became depressed. Depression is not an indelible part of my makeup, and after two days I knew that I had to create a way to overcome these new demons. I was a writer. I was going to write. But I could not live as a writer, riddled with the anxiety that had come to be associated with having my work enter the public sphere, which is exactly where I wanted it to be.

My meditation practice didn't feel sufficient to go to this new place and space that I longed for. Then I recalled my former boyfriend's practice. He had needed therapy (another practice I had adopted) in addition to those periods of silence, yet I remembered that he often "came out" of those periods of silence in some ways more emotionally accessible.

I wanted to find joy not only in writing my books but in launching them into the world and being a member of the writing community, a community that so often fueled and fanned, and encouraged the toxic emotions I was feeling. I began spending weekends in silence at Pendle Hill, a Quaker retreat center outside of Philadelphia. I was only forty-five minutes from Philadelphia in Wallingford, Pennsylvania, yet on the twenty-three-acre campus I felt I was in another world.

During my first weekend silent retreat at Pendle Hill, I learned that silence is so many things. Silence is calm and soothing, but it is also active and dynamic. The energy that I would have expended in talking and expressing the emotions that accompany conversation found a resting and a nesting place within me. As I took long walks around the campus, joined the group for short periods of meditation, ate with the group in silence, napped in my room, journaled, read, and actively tried to harness a contemplative mindset, I was blessedly relieved of the sound of my voice. Silence introduced me to what I often overlook or ignore. How my body moves. The rhythm of my walk. The sound of my breathing. The feel of the sun or wind on my skin. Ideas stuffed into the corners of my mind shook off the cobwebs and stepped forth. The downtime of silence always lifts me.

Experiencing the respect for silence that is built into the Quaker practice and walking the woods and pathways around the campus, I got lost and I got found. Sitting in my small room I journaled, prayed, cried, meditated, and listened to my heart. These retreats where I was silent but actively being and listening enlarged my soul.

✦ ✦ ✦

With the will and commitment to deeply know yourself and use that knowledge as a springboard to healing every day, it is possible to create pockets of stillness and joy in your life, no matter the circumstances of your life. You may be afraid of stillness and quiet because it is inevitably filled with memories of unhealed, unacknowledged wounds and trauma. You can't be still or quiet because that state of mind is hijacked by a past that still haunts and cripples you. You should then seek counseling or mental health support. Seek the advice of a friend who has had the experience of working on her mental health in this way. Talk to a trusted friend who never steers you wrong. Pray on it or meditate on it through the din and the noise that threatens to capsize the yearning for peace of mind and your heart will show you the way.

You're a single mother, a woman working three jobs, a stressed-out executive, or a woman in a relationship with a partner who you feel neither recognizes nor supports your deepest emotional needs. Or you're just feeling increasingly overwhelmed. It's time to get real. It's time to get honest, first with yourself and then with others. Once you recognize that you need downtime, me time, quiet time, share that with those closest to you. This is not an admission of weakness or failure but the first step in becoming more healthy, more loving of yourself and others, and in all the ways that matter to you, more "powerful." Let all these folks know that this is your new project. A project that you need their support to complete. And you complete it every day. This is a joy project, a life-saving project. They don't have to understand you, just support you. And if they can't support you, **you** can be all the support you need.

Ask a friend or family member to care for your child or children so you can have "downtime." You're not running an errand. You're not **doing something**. You have a date with yourself. Promise to do the same for them when they need the same. Many days I wake up and tell my husband I am taking a **me day**. Maybe I will choose to be silent for much of the day. Maybe I will treat myself to a movie and lunch or a museum **alone**. This has been an integral part of our thirty-plus-year marriage since the beginning of our union, and Joe is neither threatened nor confused by my **me days**. He relishes the results of my downtime. When I'm out of the house, he can play his music and play the piano as loud as he wants; while I'm thinking my thoughts and connecting with my soul, he is indirectly doing the same. And he has a happy wife.

Start your day fifteen, ten minutes, or half an hour early, and just be quiet and still before your feet hit the floor. You can use the time to plan your day, or you can use the time to simply breathe in and out and let your mind go *wherever*.

If you need to spend more time away from your friends, "hanging out" and partying less, talk to your friends about this. Let them know that you are not rejecting them but trying to find new ways to be yourself. And sometimes that means being *by yourself*. You may find that your desire echoes the unexpressed needs of your friends as well.

Be specific in your ask. Do you need your partner to take over more of the household chores so you can have more chill time when you can home from work? Say that. Would you like your partner to go for a walk with you? Ask that.

If your living space is small, put a Do Not Disturb sign on the door or a room you have chosen for your pockets of stillness and quiet. You have the right to do that.

Walk with your friends but also walk alone so that you can look at the trees, hear yourself think, and look, really look, at the sky. Walk without your earbuds. Instead of listening to someone else's story, listen to your own. Being in nature and *not doing anything* reduces stress and improves mood. If there are no parks or trees in your community find an area where they are and go there often.

If you do not feel safe walking in your community research recreation centers or walking paths in other neighborhoods.

Find ways in the middle of the day to slow down and be still for five or ten minutes. Even a five-minute break especially done more than once can have a powerful and positive impact on mind/body health. Many workplaces will allow employees to take a five-to-twenty-minute smoke break. Five to twenty minutes to ingest toxins! In an increasing number of professional settings, employers have introduced nap rooms that can be used for mid-day breaks. Take and make your own break.

- Download a meditation or calming app on your phone.
- Start email-free days.
- Turn your phone off.

Curate what you consume on social media, in films, TV, and streaming. The relentless "*Cops killing*

Black people" or "*Crazed Walmart employee massacres coworkers*" videos are images I avoid. I can't block out all the news. I don't even want to, but I can control how much I consume and decide that I don't have to watch murder and mayhem on repeat. That small decision is a big decision that supports my emotional equilibrium.

For me, all of this is about joy. **Joy!** I guard my joy with my life, and I sustain it with my practices. I don't let anyone, **anyone**, threaten it. If they do, then something has to change. My joy is not being happy because of anything that has happened; it is a state of mind that I work hard to infuse into my life. *It ain't easy.* I practice it every day. I have yet to master it, but I practice it. I practice it when, during my morning meditation I visualize people in my life, including myself, my family and friends, and especially those who provide me with the most frequent spiritual "growth opportunities" all gathered in an open field beneath a spring shower. In this visualization the raindrops are huge and inside each raindrop, I can see the word *love*. All of our faces are poised skyward, and we are laughing in amazement and joy. I give myself and those in my life a love bath. The image of that shower of affection and grace makes me smile and laugh, and it helps me through my day. This acts as my energy. It's like the Serenity Prayer 5.0.

Quiet, stillness, me time, and meditation, again and again, give me back to myself.

Give me a better version of myself.

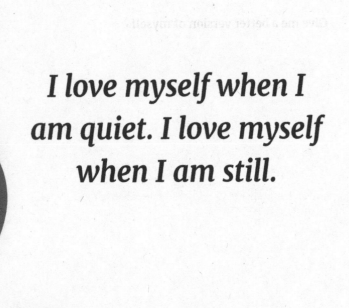

I love myself when I am quiet. I love myself when I am still.

**Silence isn't empty;
it's full of answers.**

Listen to silence.

It has so much to say.

—RUMI

PART II

Say Hello to Yourself

"Caring for myself is not self-indulgence, it is self-preservation, and that is an act of political warfare."

—AUDRE LORDE

In the silence, you meet yourself. Your secret self, your sister self. You meet her in a way that is deeply personal and restorative because you are meeting her alone. In the silence, in meditation, in taking long walks alone, you get to hear her voice. You get to hear her voice, which is your voice, and it sharpens your intuition, it sharpens your knowing, and it sharpens your ability to know what you need to know. Hearing this voice sharpens your ability to know what you need to do. We often look far and wide, seeking answers outside ourselves, but we know the answers; we are just not ready to embrace them, reveal them, and hold on to them. We fear rousing the answers into powerful wakefulness.

My years of engaging in contemplative practices have made me smarter and more emotionally intelligent. Our feelings are a form of intelligence. And yet I know I must habitually practice this form of emotional self-care. *I wash my face. I brush my teeth. I am mindful. I say hello to me.* Each day I am slaying my demons, battling my doubts. I am adequately armed, but I still have obsessive, irrelevant, and sometimes fearful thoughts. But I meet them head-on. I take back my mind. *So, say hello to yourself.* It takes time and dedication, but learning how to see the small things outside us and inside of us allows us to see and feel and understand everything around us and gives us the courage to grow. Your inner sister is a reflection of you. Water her like a flower. Water her through acts of self-support, self-discovery, and self-imposed rest and relaxation. Go on a date with yourself. Going inside is a miraculous journey that is surprising, and you will meet a wonderful person. A person who is braver than you could have imagined, more tender and surprising and beautiful than you were prepared for. Don't be afraid, her radiance will not harm you; it will merely lift you onto the shores of your private heaven.

Secrets to a Long and Happy Life:

◊ Move naturally and regularly.

◊ Exercise.

◊ Find your life's purpose.

◊ Relax and relieve stress.

◊ Build a social network.

◊ Have faith.

◊ Love your body and care for it.

◊ Recognize that your mental health is as important as your physical health.

"One needs occasionally to stand aside from the hum and rush of human interests and passions to hear the voice of God."

—ANNA JULIA COOPER, TEACHER, WRITER, AND ACTIVIST WHO LIVED TO THE AGE OF 105

"Breathing through something, engaging in some deep reflection, allows us to see the give-and-take of life... Like physical breathing, reflection clears the mind."

—EARTHA KITT,
ACTRESS, DANCER, SINGER,
TEACHER OF DANCE, ACTIVIST

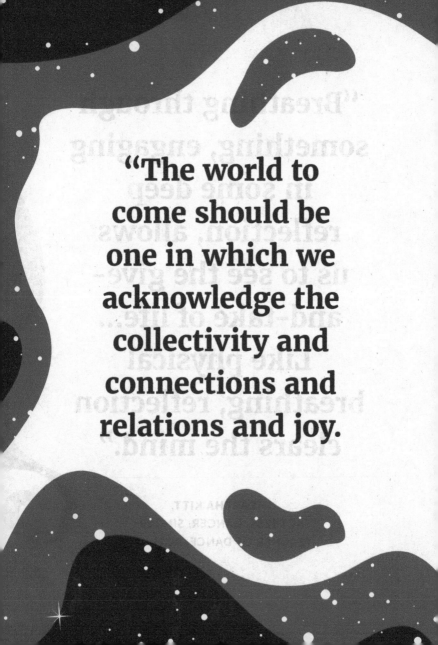

"The world to come should be one in which we acknowledge the collectivity and connections and relations and joy.

If we don't start practicing collective self-care now, there's no way to imagine, much less reach, a time of freedom."

—ANGELA DAVIS,
AUTHOR, ACTIVIST, PHILOSOPHER,
AND FEMINIST

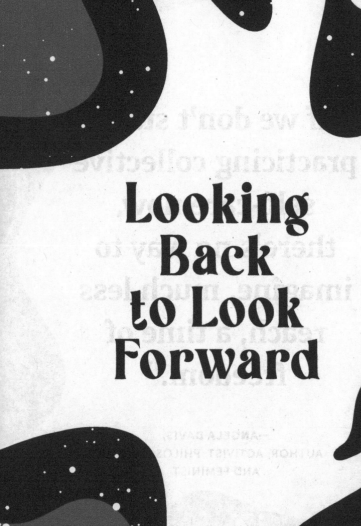

Looking Back to Look Forward

African-descended women have a centuries-old tradition of going within, contemplating, and communicating with the spirits seen and unseen to infuse their lives with harmony and inner peace. These practices flourished even during the storms of enslavement, war, colonialism, and the abuse of Black women's bodies. We have worshiped the Yoruba God Oshun, called the river orisha, or goddess, in the Yoruba religion and who is typically associated with water, purity, fertility, love, and sensuality. We created hoodoo, Voudon, and Santeria to cleanse our spirits and release the toxicity of the wounds inflicted on us by situations beyond our control. When you go into the silence when you meditate as a Black woman you are calling up and calling on spirits that are part of your cultural, historical, and ancestral inheritance. Too many of us have been separated from practices that our mothers were conditioned to feel were a natural and significant part of their lives. Whether we practice yoga or mindfulness, prayer, or Santería we affirm the presence of the One God active in our lives and affairs. The One God is multi-lingual and multicultural and belongs to us all. My spiritual practice is an ever-turning wheel, a mosaic of influences welcoming me home each time I claim them.

Using the power of prayer, Black women:

Protected their children

Blessed themselves and others

Envisioned the realization of their dreams

Overcame disease

Rose from poverty

Transcended misery

Fought injustice

In the African American Christian tradition, the image of a Black woman praying is perhaps the most indelible. More powerful even, than the image of the preacher holding forth in the pulpit. Many of our mothers weave and wove prayer into a language of sustenance and survival. They made the Bible an instruction manual for life and turned the church into a place where they found solace and redemption, despite being too often silenced and marginalized behind its doors. For these women, prayer is medicine and therapy. Prayer is the backbone that enables them to stand tall in their minds and stride through the minefields dotting their lives. Silent prayer. Out loud prayer. Shouting prayer. Singing prayer. Joyous prayer. Humble prayer. Confused and desperate prayer. Prayer is the road Black women have walked toward peace and joy. And then there are the Black women who have preached, healed, christened, and baptized, sanctified and anointed by their connection to the profound message of love given to them by their concept and experience of God.

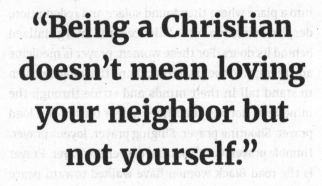

"Being a Christian doesn't mean loving your neighbor but not yourself."

—DR. AUDREY CHAPMAN

"And I remember people coming to my mother's yard to be given cuttings from her flowers: I hear again the praise showered on her because whatever rocky soil she landed on, she turned into a garden. A garden so brilliant with colors, so original in its design, so magnificent with life and creativity, that to this day people drive by our house in Georgia— perfect strangers and imperfect strangers—and ask to stand or walk among my mother's art.

"I notice it is only when my mother is working on her flowers that she is radiant, almost to the point of being invisible—except as Creator: hand and eye. She is involved in work her soul must have. Ordering the universe in the image of her personal conception of Beauty."

—ALICE WALKER,
FROM *IN SEARCH OF OUR MOTHERS' GARDENS: WOMANIST PROSE*

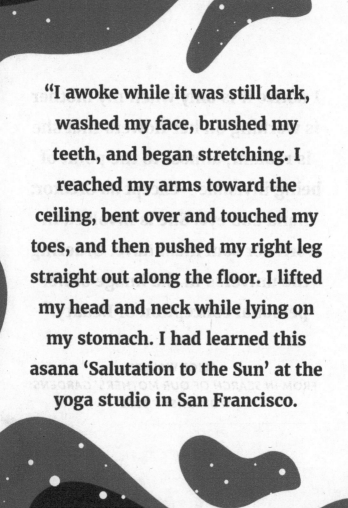

"I awoke while it was still dark, washed my face, brushed my teeth, and began stretching. I reached my arms toward the ceiling, bent over and touched my toes, and then pushed my right leg straight out along the floor. I lifted my head and neck while lying on my stomach. I had learned this asana 'Salutation to the Sun' at the yoga studio in San Francisco.

As I flowed into the movements, I awakened fully to my inner connection with the unknown. An orb of peace radiated in my chest, and I relaxed into the awareness that God's radiant spirit cared for me and held my energy in the universe."

—DEBORAH SANTANA,
FROM *SPACE BETWEEN THE STARS: MY JOURNEY TO AN OPEN HEART*

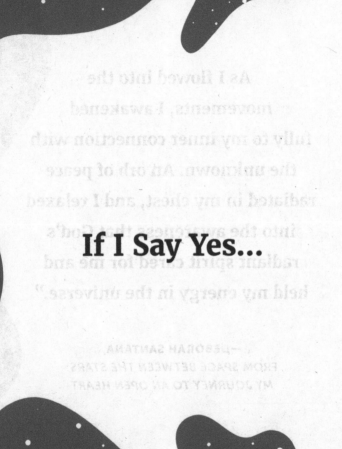

If I Say Yes...

If I Say No...

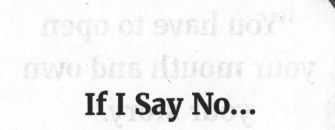

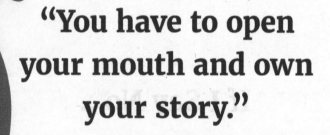

"You have to open your mouth and own your story."

—VIOLA DAVIS,
EGOT AWARD-WINNING ACTOR

The New Black Woman is at her most courageous, healthy, and impressive when she confidently and with no apology sets boundaries. I think I was born with a fully activated *no* gene. Maybe it's because I cherished private time to write and read and aggressively protected that time. Maybe it was seeing my mother say *no* to an unfulfilling marriage more than once. Maybe it was coming of age during the Civil Rights, Black Power, and Women's Rights movements. Likely the impact of all of those strengthened my ability to say *no* when I wanted to.

The New Black Woman relishes making time for herself and making that time Prime Time. She understands that saying *no* to what she doesn't want to do, what she feels is not in her best interest, or what may harm her is an act of integrity, survival, and self-love. She understands that saying *no* to a request that those asking could easily perform empowers them to use their imagination and intelligence in problem-solving. She understands that if she is to be respected by family, friends, and coworkers they must respect and value her time and not take it for granted.

PART III

No Is Not a
Bad Word

Black women are stereotyped as never at a loss for words. As being women who always have something to say. As saying what we want to say whether others want to hear it or not. But are we saying what we need to say? Are we saying what we want to say? Language can be a shield, a preemptive strike, or a purposeful misdirection. If we are expected to always be strong, we may feel we must always be right. And right then becomes what others say it is or what others need "right" to be. Our families often censor what we can express and how honest we can be. Our jobs require we "present" and "show up" in prescribed ways. If we are trapped in a toxic love relationship, we can find ourselves performing in exchange for what only sporadically feels like love. And if we dare speak our truth in these situations all that we hold dear, acceptance, respect, and affection, may be on the line.

When we can't chisel the words that will free or authenticate us, we turn to actions. We shut down verbally to punish others. Flee a job or relationship and let our absence do the talking.

Because so many of us have not given ourselves permission to say no and mean it and to say yes and see that as an act of affirmation, we find our lives cluttered with people and activities, commitments and obligations that stymie and sabotage us. But before we can say yes to ourselves and no to others, we have to see both words as ours to possess, shape, and mold rather than language we are borrowing from others that has to meet their conditions. I have spent my life learning the beauty of yes and the power of no, the power of yes and the beauty of no.

Traditionally, women are only supposed to say yes to anyone who asks anything of them. But tradition has been reworked and revised so much over the generations that no one has that expectation anymore, right? Not quite. Especially in Black families, where women are disproportionately anchor and backbone, no is taboo, no is an insult, and no is tantamount to going AWOL. This fear that we will lose love, family, and ourselves even if we say no is deeply embedded and hard to dislodge. But dislodge it we must. To find ourselves. To be ourselves. To love ourselves.

"Loving yourself is the very first thing. Love yourself. Take care of yourself. Many of the women who come to see me were never taken care of by their mothers so they have no idea how to 'mother' themselves. That means they are clueless about how to set boundaries. They may have had to parent other younger siblings starting at a young age and 'mother' others but were never mothered themselves.

Many women will need therapy to learn how to set boundaries. Black women are told that their grandmothers or mothers didn't complain, bore every weight, and solved every problem and so they have to carry on that tradition. Black women have the right to set limits. You don't have to always be the first responder in any crisis."

—DR. AUDREY CHAPMAN

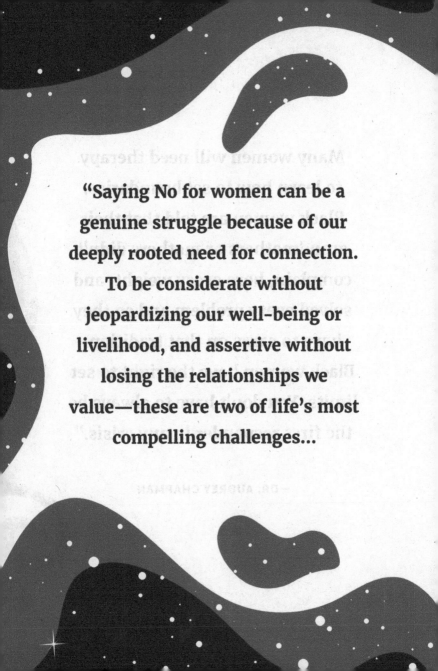

"Saying No for women can be a genuine struggle because of our deeply rooted need for connection. To be considerate without jeopardizing our well-being or livelihood, and assertive without losing the relationships we value—these are two of life's most compelling challenges...

Women's reluctance to say NO comes from traits that we should value—empathy, sensitivity, thoughtfulness, and compassion rather than suppress when saying NO. These traits are necessary elements of human connection and preservation."

—NANETTE GARTRELL,
FROM *MY ANSWER IS NO...IF THAT'S OKAY WITH YOU: HOW WOMEN CAN SAY NO AND (STILL) FEEL GOOD ABOUT IT*

When dealing with family or friends living with untreated trauma, profound emotional stress, or mental illness getting to *no* may require seeking the support of a professional counselor. For most situations, Nanette Gartrell gives the following advice when setting boundaries or saying *no*.

- Figure out what you're most afraid of losing.

- Remind yourself why you deserve to be treated respectfully or not taken for granted.

- Ask yourself how your life would be improved if you set limits or shut down unacceptable behavior.

- Tell yourself that you are setting boundaries to gain control over your life, confidence, and respect, not to give up a valued relationship.

Loss, Alone and in Community

Black women live in communities that are literally and figuratively often under siege, no matter the economic or class status of that community. Loss for many of us seems and feels perennial. Loss of political power, loss of agency, and disproportionate loss of loved ones are often the result of the looming legacy of systemic racism. How do we say *yes* to grief and grieving?

When I asked Dr. Pamela Brewer her thoughts about the challenges of grieving for Black women, her answer was comprehensive and compassionate. "We as a society tend to censor the grieving process. Employers are certainly known to put very specific limits on who to grieve and when to grieve and for how long. When it comes to Black women, it can be even more curtailed at the hands of colleagues and employers and we ourselves. Often, as Black women grieve, they are seen as overreacting, making an excuse to take time off from work, while a White woman could be well supported to take as much time as necessary. This is particularly the case when the cause of the grief is considered appropriate, for example, an illness or addiction that is deemed acceptable or understandable or violence that is not blamed on the victim."

For a Black woman, however, the response, the compassionate embrace needed at a time of grief is often unavailable. If the cause of the grief is seen as socially unacceptable (murder, murder by police, drug/addiction/poverty-related, or "her fault"), there can be a smaller pool of understanding and acceptance from which to draw support.

What is also true, and often overlooked, is that as Black women we experience small and large loss/grief episodes as part of our daily experience—socially, politically, economically, professionally, educationally, financially. Loss...grief...it's the daily lens through which we work to squeeze out some semblance of a healthy life—despite the daily grind of loss. When that grief is exacerbated by losing a loved one, regardless of how "close" that loved one is, the grieving process is more complex.

For Black women the loss of another Black body, a close one, or a person, miles away is so enveloping, often overwhelming, sadly so commonplace that there can be an instinctive tendency to shut it down/wall it off/do the "Strong Black Woman" dance to continue the daily duties of life. And isn't that traumatic learning what we learned through our ancestors' lives? A way to survive was to put the pain in a box and continue to work. Because, truly, to let in the horror of it all was to/ is to take one's breath away. But when we don't let our grief in, allow it to be felt in the kaleidoscope of ways in which we feel, when we do not allow ourselves the gift of healthy grieving and we try to send the grief underground, it simply rests on another layer of grief, yet unresolved. It is hard for a wound to heal when it is continually reopened. And we continue to hurt ourselves and those around us.

Are there spaces in our community to grieve authentically? For those of us who have that "good girlfriend" or circle of girlfriends, or even a close male friend, there can be tremendous solace. But then again the myths of grieving ("you just need to get over it," "it's been XX months," "it's time for you to move on," "you are young; you can have another," and so much more that people often unknowingly express, say, or believe) along with the reality of daily life often force Black women in particular to grieve when there is time, and that time is never found. So, we must find and create it in whatever amazing and creative ways work for us, including setting limits.

Take a ridiculously long shower and take a break from all your devices—you know how to figure it out. Creating "talking circles" can be helpful and healing and freeing and empowering, all at the same time. Particularly during the grieving process it is important to treat ourselves as we would a dear friend, someone we love and care about—someone we treasure.

When I Said
Yes to Me

I left my first marriage because I felt trapped and unseen. Muted and ignored. My yes was formed not in one fell swoop but over many days and months. Truth be told, it was formed over years, years in which I swallowed it, shouted over its voice, and locked it in a soundproof room. I am a person who values honesty but when deceit and lies became the only way I felt I could find space to breathe I knew I had to say yes to me. Yes to a me I had not yet met; yes to a me I did not know or even recognize but into whose profile and form and shape I was steadily growing. *Yes* took hold of me in strange, funny ways, masquerading as depression and misery, making me feel I was two people torn asunder and that I might never be whole. *Yes* does not come to you easily. Sometimes yes is brutal and demanding, a slap across the face. Because once we say *yes* we can't ever go back to the moment before we said it. If I said yes to this strange necessary woman I had to be beyond and outside the borders of my marriage, there was no going back to the day before I said yes to her. Even if I tried.

Everything before yes was now suspect. The puzzle pieces would no longer fit. I knew I had to say yes to whatever lay ahead because where I was felt like a life sentenced to an emptiness I would never fill.

Yes is leaping and sometimes falling off a cliff. *Yes* is discovering once you land that you are buoyant and maybe you can even fly. *Yes* is, "I have no choice but to call on strength that at this moment I don't believe I have but my faith tells me is there." *Yes* is scary, like all the choices that release our courage and the warrior angel inside of us. Say yes to you.

When I Said Yes to Me (Again)

When I write my books, I say yes to myself. I am saying yes to my imagination, unique story, opinions, and desire to connect with others through stories. When I am creating a writing project and allowing that project to create me, I have to say yes over and over. I have to say yes when there are things I don't know. I say yes to the possibility and likelihood that in time I will know those things. I have to say yes when my internal censor (I still have one) warns me, "Don't go there." But in writing and creating, *there* is where you want to go. *There* is the messy swamp of secrets and lies and things unsaid and unimagined because somebody said all that stuff, all that *there* is off-limits. Good writing, powerful creation, is saying yes, again and again, to break through the nos. That is why my writing gives me so much life. I don't just say yes, or create yes, but through the process of writing a story I have to open myself to yes to receive it and welcome it to a home in my spirit.

We all are creative. We all have a passion gestating within us, longing to be born. We make excuses. There is no time. We tell ourselves stories about inevitable failure, are afraid to risk exposure, and hear what we fear will be the negative opinions of others. (We never imagine positive opinions.) Perhaps we fear that bearing the weight of our brilliance would destroy us. We are stronger than we ever imagine.

Unearth your buried passion, hobby, or interest and shape it into a yes.

Setting Boundaries for Self-Healing

Two of the most beloved and cherished heroines/ heroes of the canon of literature that African American women writers have created are Celie in Alice Walker's award-winning novel *The Color Purple* and Maya Angelou in her memoir *I Know Why the Caged Bird Sings*. In *The Color Purple*, fourteen-year-old Celie is a victim of rape, poverty, sexism, and racism, a poor Black girl who has been ground into the dust of self-hatred and fear. But while Celie is repeatedly told no in the novel, she chisels her way into a resounding yes for herself, her life, and her ability to love. The novel is written as a series of letters that begin with letters to God. Although Celie cannot speak of her shame and trauma with those around her, she affirms her right to speak and be heard in the novel. She speaks through letters. Letters that are "written" but could just as well have been prayed or silently spoken to a God Celie knows lives within her.

In *I Know Why the Caged Bird Sings*, after she was raped at the age of eight by her mother's boyfriend, Maya told her family what had happened to her. The man was arrested, tried, convicted, and jailed for one day. When he was released from prison her uncles beat the man to death. For the next six years, Maya was mute. Angelou wrote that she refused to speak because she had come to believe that her words and her voice had killed a man. I have also long believed that Maya, as a victim of rape, trauma, post-traumatic stress disorder, guilt, and shame, stopped speaking to say yes to herself. She chose silence to heal, nurse, and nurture her battered soul. The adults around her could not protect her from sexual molestation, likely had no words to reach her battered soul, and then in an act that the community saw as "just," ensnared Maya in taking the life of a man.

How would, how could Maya find words to speak to anyone but her beloved brother Bailey with whom she periodically shared her deepest feelings? In her silence, selective, chosen, and imposed Maya said yes to herself and no to those who had even though they loved her had been unable to keep her safe. Her silence was a loud yes. There are times when silence is a powerful form of speech. Maya was hoarding her strength, living a life of her mind and feelings, and putting herself back together again, saying yes to herself only.

"For Black women, it is often a badge of honor to sacrifice ourselves. We buy into neglecting ourselves because we are 'giving back.' And giving back makes us feel good and it makes us feel powerful. It feels good to know that all these people need you.

But when you are consistently saying yes when you want to say no you end up feeling physically and emotionally drained, resentful, and bitter. You are hiding your pain behind a smile. You are laying the seeds also for physical ailments caused by emotional stress. I tell my clients to Say no. Say no not right now. Say I can't do what you ask but I can do something else."

Setting boundaries makes space for you. Many Black women fear that personal space because they fear it will be filled with the sounds of their inner demons and pain. They feel that in that private personal space, all they will hear and feel will be negative. If there was one thing I would tell Black women to do for their mental health, it would be to "slow down."

Slow down so you can hear your deepest needs; slow down so you can say no if no brings you peace of mind and joy and is an authentic statement about who you are. No is an act of liberation.

Setting boundaries and slowing down has to become a "practice" that you "practice" every day. You will have to negotiate with close family members; you will have to "train" family members and friends used to always hearing you say yes, that you have decided to sometimes say no. Appreciate that they will need time to accept the "new you." But stand up for and protect the new life options grounded in mental health that you are carving out for yourself. Just as it will take time for you to master this new consciousness, it will take time for others to accept it. But honor and protect your deepest needs.

PART IV

My Body/
My Self

The New Black Woman possesses a new and radically positive relationship with her body and her health.

The New Black Woman refuses to be a victim of or practice colorist beliefs about her skin color, whether she is dark or light.

The New Black Woman acknowledges that Black women glory in a concept of beauty and physical size that includes big bodies. The New Black Woman, however, ensures her health with regular checkups and a healthy lifestyle to avoid diabetes or obesity, two diseases that are precursors of heart disease, stroke, and dementia.

The New Black Woman has regular physical checkups and seeks mental health support when needed. Her relationship with her healthcare providers is one where she feels listened to and respected.

The New Black Woman guides and supports her family in talking honestly and openly about illness, death, and dying and models these conversations for her children.

The New Black Woman recognizes that her relationships with family, friends, and coworkers can sustain or undermine her health. If those relationships are toxic, she seeks to repair them. She understands that she may need to seek advice to develop healing strategies. If she feels broken by a relationship, she attempts to repair that brokenness, holds everyone involved in the light, and holds onto her joy. She releases and accepts what she cannot change.

The New Black Woman cherishes her body. She moves, exercises, and relishes stillness and rest.

The New Black Woman has "sister circles" of women friends who nurture her strength, accept and appreciate her vulnerabilities, and reinforce her best instincts about her life and life choices.

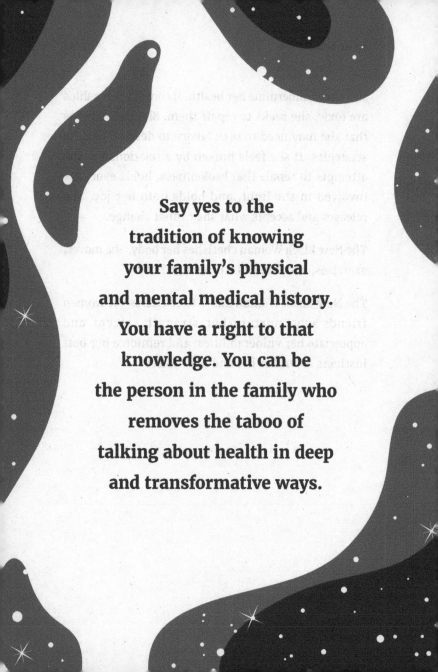

Say yes to the tradition of knowing your family's physical and mental medical history. You have a right to that knowledge. You can be the person in the family who removes the taboo of talking about health in deep and transformative ways.

Prioritizing Physical Health

The Strong Black Woman complex imposes a dangerous separation of Black women from their bodies. We know about the mind/body connection, the belief that the causes, development, and outcomes of a physical illness are determined by the interaction of psychological, social, and biological factors. Too many Black women suffer from a mind–body disconnect. Because so many of us possess minds that repeatedly tell us that we must be strong, be in charge, and have no time for weakness, our minds sabotage our health. We need minds that are a portal for monologues that inspire us, not dictate to us. Train yourself to know that the mind talks to the body and the body talks to the mind. The body is a single unit (body, mind, soul, and spirit acting in tandem) encompassing, influenced, and affected by all we do. The stories we tell ourselves are a factor in creating the lives we live.

We hear our bodies asking for help as we suffer insomnia, weight gain, weight loss, irritability, high blood pressure, loss of energy, headaches, and depression and too often we silence the voice of pain; we censor it, we excise it.

Black women are living in a health emergency intensified by the daily assaults of systemic racism.

Part of that health emergency is lodged in this statistic too: In America each day four Black women are murdered by a spouse, domestic partner, or lover. Violence, deadly violence, must be acknowledged as part of the health emergency we face.

Heart disease is the leading cause of death in America. It is the leading cause of death for Black women. The definition of a Strong Black Woman is a woman who gives her heart away. She gives her heart away and asks nothing in return. She gives her heart to others and feels no sense of depletion or buries anger when her requests for heart-inspired support are rejected or ignored. The traditional, old-school Strong Black Woman tells herself that is the price of being loved and needed. But we need to think about our hearts as though they were newborn babies we are holding in our arms, a bouquet we have not expected, or the feel of the hand of someone we love who loves us.

We must cherish our hearts because they are and symbolize our center, our core.

We must care for our hearts, make them strong, and give our hearts metaphorically only to those who will cherish them as we do.

✦ ✦ ✦

The bodies of Black women in America have endured so much, the physical punishments and abuse of enslavement, which included rape, malnutrition as a result of poverty, lack of access to good medical care as a result of segregation, involuntary sometimes forced sterilization, and the unique shape and size of our bodies cited as "ugly." Yet we are a new generation. A generation taking back self-esteem, redefining the meaning of strength with voices and conviction that spring from the muted stories of female ancestors and the stories our female ancestors dared to speak. We have led movements for human and civil rights, traveled into space, given music new sounds and dimensions and literature bold vision, discovered cures for disease, and been the heart of our often-battered communities. We are lion-hearted women. But even the hearts of lions need to be tended.

A Mindset of
Positivity

I use affirmations like this one
to create a mindset of health:

Through the power and presence
of the Divine mind active in my
life and active through me,

I affirm that I am a loving steward
of my mind, body, and soul.

I claim loving health-giving
attitudes, thoughts, and beliefs
that connect me to the needs of
my mind, body, and soul.

I say *yes* to healing,

I say *yes* to health,

I say *yes* to expressing and being
My most beautiful and
productive self.

I am willing to break in order to
be repaired.

I listen to my pain and respect
its message.

I have the courage to be well.

As the sun rises,
I say *yes* to me.

With each breath,
I say *yes* to me.

As the sun sets,
I say *yes* to me.

Final Thoughts

In the opening pages of this book, I asked you to practice silence and introspection. I risked making you uncomfortable by asking unexpected, difficult questions. Perhaps when initially encountering a question, you thought, "No way I can answer that" and then realized you could. I hope these pages inspired you to think about your mind, body, and spirit. How precious they are how much they give you and how skillfully and tenderly you must care for them. I wrote this book because I am still learning to love myself, ever more fiercely and perfectly each day. I am on this journey with you. I still have questions, more questions than answers. I thank Mother/God for the questions. Questions make me brave, illuminate the path to truth, and keep me growing when I have erroneously convinced myself that "I have arrived." I asked you so many questions because Black women are not asked enough questions about the state of their minds, bodies, and spirits. And the most important questions are: What are you willing to do to ensure your health? Who are you willing to become? Are you brave enough to become the New Black Woman?

Resource
Guide

Welcome to our resource guide for Black women.

This guide is a collection of resources meant to empower and uplift Black women looking to prioritize their well-being and personal growth—women who recognize that they often bear the weight of multiple responsibilities and the pressure to succeed in a world that doesn't always value us.

This guide aims to center the experiences and voices of Black women so that we can explore and embrace practices of self-care, self-love, and boundary-setting while acknowledging our challenges and struggles. It provides Black women with tools and resources to help them navigate challenging situations and create spaces where they can thrive.

In this guide, we've listed resources to help you reflect on our Black experience and how it has influenced your perspectives and shaped who you are today. By exploring our personal and collective history, we hope you gain a deeper understanding of your identity as a Black woman. Looking back to look forward is one of our themes, with our resources exploring the power of reflecting on and learning from the past and the present. We invite you to acknowledge the systemic barriers, oppression, and marginalization that Black women have faced and continue to face but also recognize the incredible resilience and strength that allowed us to overcome these challenges. By leading you to reflection, the resources in this guide constitute a crucial step toward personal growth and empowerment.

This guide emphasizes, for instance, the significance of embracing silence and the art of introspection. We explore powerful resources that teach us to break from the noise and chaos of the world to achieve self-discovery and inner peace. We also delve into the practice of self-reflection, and our toolkit will help you get started and stay committed to the process. By learning to sit with ourselves and listen to our inner voice, we can gain greater clarity and direction in our lives.

We also explore the significance of setting boundaries in our personal and professional lives. We examine ways to heal and grow as individuals and as a community by creating supportive networks and advocating for our needs. By prioritizing our well-being and fostering a sense of community, we can empower ourselves and others to achieve personal and collective growth.

Some sections in this guide deeply dive into the intricate relationship between our bodies and our sense of self. We must prioritize our physical health as it is crucial to our overall well-being. We provide various resources to achieve this—resources about exercise, healthy eating, and self-care practices that cater to our individual needs as Black women. Beyond physical health, we provide resources that delve into the psychological aspect of well-being to help you develop a positive mindset that can help cultivate joy in your life. Many of these tools help you understand and appreciate your body for what it is so that you may develop a more loving relationship with yourself. This guide is designed to empower you to take control of your physical and mental health and to help you live a happier and healthier life.

May you be reminded that Black women deserve to prioritize their own well-being and personal growth. As we often carry the weight of our communities and the world on our shoulders, it can be easy to neglect our needs. We hope this guide inspires and empowers you on your journey toward self-care and self-discovery.

May it give you the tools and resources to cultivate a healthy, joyful, and fulfilling life. Remember that you deserve love, care, and attention; we hope this guide helps you prioritize those things for yourself.

M.J. Fievre, author of *Badass Black Girl*

Marita Golden, author of *The Strong Black* Woman, *Saving Our Sons*, and *The New Black Woman*

✦ ✦ ✦

RESOURCES
APPS FOR SELF-CARE AND SELF-DISCOVERY

Self-care and self-discovery are essential components of mental and emotional well-being. These apps offer various tools and resources to help Black women navigate the complexities of their identities and experiences, find peace, and develop a positive relationship with themselves. From guided meditations to access to culturally competent therapists, these apps provide services to support users on their journeys toward greater self-awareness and self-care.

- **Ayana Therapy:** an app that matches users with culturally competent therapists who understand their unique identities and experiences. Users can choose from various categories such as race, ethnicity, gender identity, sexual orientation, religion, etc.

- **Calm:** a meditation and mindfulness app that offers guided meditations, sleep stories, and other relaxation tools.

- **Exhale:** an innovative emotional well-being application tailored to the needs of Black women and women of color. With a range of features such as affirmations, guided visualizations, breathing exercises, and meditations, this app promotes relaxation and positive self-talk.

- **Insight Timer:** a free meditation app that offers guided meditations, music, and talks on mindfulness and self-care.

- **Liberate Meditation:** an app designed to help Black, Indigenous, and people of color practice mindfulness and meditation. The app offers guided meditations, talks, and daily reminders to help users stay present and centered.

- **Melanin and Mental Health:** an app that connects users with culturally competent and compassionate therapists who understand the unique needs of Black women. Along with therapy services, the app offers a podcast, a blog, and events celebrating Black mental health.

- **Real:** an app that works as a personalized mental health membership and helps users work on their emotional health goals. It offers live group sessions, on-demand therapy tools, curated content, and expert guidance.

- **Sad Girls Club:** an app that serves as a community for women of color who struggle with mental health issues. It provides online support groups, workshops, events, and content that promote healing and wellness.

- **(The) Safe Place:** a mental health app for the Black community that offers a wealth of resources, information, statistics, and tips on coping with mental health issues such as depression, anxiety, PTSD, and racism.

- **Shine App:** an app created by a Black woman and focused on self-care for people of color. It offers guided meditations, daily affirmations, and other tools for mindfulness. *The Daily Shine* is a daily self-care and mindfulness newsletter created by the founders of Shine App, specifically for Black women.

- **Sista Afya:** a mental wellness app created by Black women for Black women. It provides online therapy sessions, support groups, workshops, webinars, and resources that foster healing and community.

MORE APPS FOR BLACK WOMEN

In addition to the self-care and mental health apps we previously mentioned, many other mobile applications are designed to empower and support Black women. From fitness and beauty to journaling and networking, these apps offer a range of tools and resources to help Black women thrive in all aspects of life.

- **EatOkra3:** an app that helps users discover Black-owned eateries in their locality. The app was founded by a couple, Anthony and Janique Edwards, who wanted to support Black businesses and culture through food.

- **(The) Pattern:** an astrology app that analyzes users' birth charts and provides insights into their personality traits, relationships, career, and life purpose. The app also helps users understand their compatibility with others based on their behavior and communication patterns. This app helps set boundaries with people who match or clash with one's energy.

- **Tetragram:** an app designed for journaling that allows users to document their thoughts and feelings privately or share them with a supportive community. Additionally, the app enables users to track their moods, habits, and goals.

- **Cocoa Swatches:** an app that helps users find their perfect foundation shade based on their skin tone. Moreover, the app allows users to explore new makeup products and brands that cater to Black women.

- **The Plug:** an app that delivers news and insights about Black innovation and entrepreneurship. Users can stay updated on the latest trends, opportunities, and events in the Black tech ecosystem.

PODCASTS FOR SELF-CARE

Podcasts can be a powerful tool for self-care, offering an accessible way to learn, reflect, and grow. Listening to podcasts focusing on self-care, mental health, and personal development can be especially valuable for Black women, as they can provide guidance and support that speaks to their unique experiences and challenges. In this list, we've gathered some of the best podcasts for Black women looking to prioritize their well-being and cultivate a positive mindset. From expert interviews to personal stories and practical advice, these podcasts cover various topics and approaches to help you on your self-care journey.

- *Balanced Black Girl Podcast*: a podcast about health, happiness, and daily life challenges— offers women of color a refreshing take on wellness.

- *Black Girls in Om*: a podcast that explores wellness, self-care, and self-love from the perspective of Black women. It's one of the tools offered by the virtual community of the same name, which provides resources and events on self-care, wellness, and mindfulness specifically for Black women.

- *(The) Friend Zone*: a podcast hosted by three friends, which discusses mental health, self-care, and personal growth.

- *Resilient Black Women*: a podcast hosted by the founders of the nonprofit Resilient Black Women; they offer guided meditations, interviews, and stories that inspire courage and healing for Black women.

- *Soul Sistas Sleep Meditations*: meditation sessions designed to cater to the needs of Black, indigenous, and women of color from all parts of the world; this podcast helps you reconnect with your inner self and achieve a state of peace and tranquility.

- *She Explores*: a platform that shares the stories of women exploring the outdoors and traveling.

- *Therapy for Black Girls*: a weekly podcast that discusses mental health topics and issues relevant to Black women.

PODCASTS FOR SELF-DISCOVERY

Podcasts can be a valuable tool for those seeking personal growth and self-discovery. Whether you're looking for inspiration, guidance, or a new perspective on life, there's a podcast for you. In this list, we've compiled some of the best podcasts for Black women who want to explore their inner selves, find their purpose, and live their best lives. From interviews with thought leaders and experts to personal stories and reflections, these podcasts offer a wealth of insights and wisdom to help you on your journey of self-discovery.

- *Black Joy Mixtape*: a podcast featuring conversations about Black joy and creativity, with a focus on the experiences of Black women.

- *(The) Black Tech Unplugged Podcast*: a podcast that explores the experiences of Black people in the tech industry.

- *Black Women Travel Podcast*: a podcast that shares travel stories and tips with a focus on the experiences of Black women.

- *Black Women's Voices*: a podcast that amplifies the voices and experiences of Black women.

- *Gettin' Grown*: a podcast that discusses everything that Black women are talking about in a hilarious way.

- *Hear to Slay*: a podcast that offers insightful commentary on politics and popular culture from a Black feminist perspective.

- *Hey, Girl*: a podcast featuring interviews with inspiring women, focusing on the stories and experiences of Black women.

- *(The) Nod*: a podcast that explores Black culture, history, and identity, focusing on lesser-known stories and perspectives.

- *Rants and Randomness*: a podcast hosted by Luvvie Ajayi, featuring interviews and conversations about culture, career, and personal growth.

- *(The) Stoop*: a storytelling podcast featuring diverse perspectives on Black identity, culture, and community.

PODCASTS FOR PHYSICAL HEALTH

Maintaining physical health is essential for overall well-being, and podcasts can be a great way to learn new tips, tricks, and information about how to take care of your body. Whether you're looking for inspiration for your next workout or advice on improving your nutrition, there's a podcast. Here are some podcasts focused on physical health that Black women may find helpful:

- *Black Girl Podcast*: a podcast that features five Black women who share their personal stories, opinions, and perspectives on various topics.

- *Black Women's Health Imperative*: a podcast hosted by Linda Goler Blount, the president and CEO of the Black Women's Health Imperative organization. It provides a particular emphasis and positive spin on Black women's health. The podcast features guests who are experts in different fields of health and wellness.

- *Black Women's Wellness*: a podcast that discusses health and wellness issues affecting Black women.

- *Brown Vegan*: a podcast hosted by Monique Koch, a vegan coach and consultant. It helps people start and maintain a vegan lifestyle. Listeners can expect practical tips, recipes, and interviews with other vegans of color.

- *(The) Motif Podcast*: a podcast that interviews women of color about their unique experiences navigating the world. Listeners can expect candid conversations and personal stories from various guests.

- *NATAL*: a podcast hosted by Martina Abrahams Ilunga and Gabrielle Horton. It explores the stories of Black birthing parents in America. The hosts and guests share their experiences, insights, and challenges related to pregnancy, birth, and parenthood.

- *(The) Wellness Collective*: a podcast hosted by Dr. Amber Thornton and Dr. Nikki Lacherza-Drew, two Black women psychologists. It explores mental health from a wellness perspective. The hosts share their insights and experiences on various topics related to mental health.

- *The Black Girl Fit Files*: a podcast that covers cross-training, pole dancing, and health and fitness topics focused on Women of Color. The host and guests discuss physical and mental health topics and the importance of representation in the fitness industry.

OTHER PODCASTS

In addition to self-care, self-discovery, and physical health, Black women may be interested in exploring many other topics through podcasts. From news and current events to pop culture and entertainment, numerous shows cater to various interests. Here are some podcasts that Black women may enjoy listening to for information, inspiration, or fun.

- *Bag Ladiez*: a podcast featuring conversations about dating, sex, and relationships from the perspective of two Black women.

- *(The) Black Girl Bravado*: a podcast featuring candid conversations about careers, love, and self-care for Black women.

- *Black Love Matters*: a podcast that discusses love, sex, and relationships from the perspective of Black couples.

- *Black Woman Leading*: a podcast dedicated to leadership development, mental wellness, and relationship management for Black women leaders in the workplace.

- *(The) Culture Soup Podcast*: a podcast that discusses diversity, equity, and inclusion in the workplace from the perspective of a Black woman.

- *(The) Sugar Jar Podcast*: a podcast featuring conversations about relationships, sex, and dating, with a focus on the experiences of Black women.

COMMUNITIES & ONLINE PLATFORMS FOR SELF-CARE AND SELF-DISCOVERY

Connecting with a community of like-minded individuals can be a powerful way to support your journey of self-care and self-discovery. These online platforms offer a variety of resources, tools, and support for Black women looking to prioritize their mental, emotional, and physical health.

- **Afrominimalist:** a platform created by a Black woman that focuses on minimalism, mindfulness, and intentional living. It offers a range of resources, including a blog, podcast, and online courses.

- **(The) Black Emotional and Mental Health Collective (BEAM):** a nonprofit organization that aims to improve the mental health and well-being of Black communities.

- **Black Girls Breathing:** a breathwork community that offers virtual sessions to release stress and trauma.

- **Black Girls with Gardens (BGWG):** a virtual community that encourages Black women to connect with nature and offers gardening and outdoor self-care resources.

- **Black Women Meditate:** an online community created to empower Black women through meditation and mindfulness. They offer a range of resources, including a free twenty-one-day meditation challenge.

- **Black Women's Yoga Collective:** a virtual community that offers yoga classes, workshops, and resources specifically for Black women.

- **Black Zen:** a community dedicated to making meditation and mindfulness accessible and relevant to Black people. They offer free guided meditations, a range of online programs, and community events.

- *For Harriet:* a blog and community focused on Black women's issues and experiences.

- **Melanin and Mental Health:** a platform dedicated to improving mental health access and support for people of color. They offer a range of resources, including a directory of therapists of color, a podcast, and various workshops and events.

- **(The) Mindful Rebel:** a platform created by a Black woman that offers resources and support for BIPOC who want to practice mindfulness. The Mindful Rebel provides online courses, workshops, and a community for like-minded individuals.

- **National Queer and Trans Therapists of Color Network:** a directory of mental health practitioners who are Black, Indigenous, or people of color and identify as queer or trans.

- **Sista Afya:** a mental wellness organization offering various programs and resources for Black women.

- **(The) Unplug Collective:** a community that offers events and resources focused on self-care and mental health for Black women.

- **(The) Well:** a digital platform that provides self-care and wellness resources for women of color.

COMMUNITIES AND ONLINE PLATFORMS FOR PHYSICAL HEALTH

Maintaining physical health is an essential aspect of self-care. Whether you're looking for workout tips or nutrition advice or want to connect with like-minded individuals who share your passion for wellness, many online communities and platforms can help. Here are some examples of communities and online platforms that Black women can join to support their physical health:

- **#MoveWithJoy:** an online fitness community that promotes joyful movement and body positivity for Black women.

- **(A)** *Black Girl's Guide to Weight Loss*: a blog that provides healthy recipes, fitness tips, and inspiration for Black women.

- **(The) Black Girl's Guide to Surviving Menopause:** a website and online community providing information and support for Black women going through menopause.

- **Black Girls Do Bike (BGDB):** a community that encourages Black women to connect with their bodies and nature through cycling.

- **Black Girls Run:** a community of Black women who encourage and support each other in achieving their fitness goals. BGR! Nation is a virtual running club for Black women that provides coaching and support.

- **Black Women Do Workout:** a website and social media community that promotes fitness and healthy living among Black women.

- **Black Women's Wellness:** a platform that offers health education, resources, and workshops for Black women.

- **Clinicians of Color:** an online directory of wellness practitioners who are people of color, specifically created to address the lack of diversity in the wellness industry.

- **FitBlackQueens:** an online community that promotes fitness, wellness, and self-care for Black women.

- **The Fit In:** a virtual community that offers fitness classes, coaching, and support for Black women.

- **GirlTrek:** a health movement encouraging Black women to walk for their physical and mental health.

- **Healthy Black Women and Girls:** an online resource for Black women interested in health and wellness, including physical fitness.

- **Planet Venus Institute:** a platform that provides health and wellness coaching for Black women.

- *Sistah Vegan:* a blog and community promoting veganism and plant-based diets among Black women.

- **Sisters in Shape:** a community of Black women passionate about fitness and wellness and supporting each other on their journeys.

- **The Yoga Green Book:** a platform that provides resources and community for Black women interested in practicing yoga.

ASSOCIATIONS & ORGANIZATIONS FOR SELF-CARE AND SELF-DISCOVERY

Many associations and organizations promote self-care and self-discovery for Black women. Whether you're looking for mental health, wellness, or personal growth resources, these groups can provide valuable support and guidance. Here are a few organizations that Black women can turn to for help and inspiration.

- **The Nap Ministry:** an organization that explores the liberating power of naps and encourages rest as a form of resistance. The Nap Ministry offers workshops, meditations, and other resources to help Black women prioritize rest and mindfulness.

- **Black Girls Rock! (BGR!):** an organization that promotes the well-being and empowerment of Black girls and women.

- **Black Mental Wellness (BMW):** an organization focusing on mental health resources and education specifically for Black individuals.

- **The Loveland Foundation:** a nonprofit organization that offers free or low-cost therapy to Black women and girls. It also provides programs, initiatives, and events that promote mental health awareness and advocacy.

- **Sisterhood Agenda:** an organization that provides resources and support for women and girls of African descent.

ASSOCIATIONS & ORGANIZATIONS FOR PHYSICAL HEALTH

Maintaining physical health is an essential part of self-care, and many associations and organizations are dedicated to promoting wellness and healthy living for Black women. These groups offer a variety of resources, from fitness classes and nutrition education to support groups and advocacy for health equity. Whether you want to improve your health or get involved in a more significant wellness movement, these associations and organizations are great places to start. Here are some examples to explore:

- **Black Mamas Matter Alliance:** a nonprofit organization dedicated to improving maternal health and well-being for Black women and their families.

- **Black Women's Health Alliance:** a nonprofit organization focused on improving the health and wellness of Black women and their families.

- **Black Women's Health Imperative:** a national organization dedicated to advancing health equity and social justice for Black women.

- **Black Women for Wellness:** a nonprofit organization that empowers Black women and girls to achieve optimal health and well-being.

- **The Body Positive:** an organization focused on promoting body acceptance and self-love for people of all sizes, including Black women.

- **The Phoenix:** a nonprofit organization that provides free sober active communities to help individuals recover from substance use disorders.

- **The Phoenix Rising Collective:** a wellness company that provides resources and coaching for Black women to embrace self-care.

- **Pretty Girls Sweat:** a nonprofit that inspires young women to prioritize their physical and mental health through fitness and wellness.

- **SoulCycle:** a fitness company that offers cycling classes and wellness programs for people of all backgrounds, including Black women.

- **The Sweat Network:** a fitness community that offers online workout classes and nutrition advice, focusing on inclusivity and diversity.

- **The Sweat Republic:** a virtual fitness community that offers group fitness classes and wellness coaching for Black women.

BOOKS FOR THE NEW BLACK WOMAN

As a Black woman, it's important to prioritize self-care, self-discovery, and personal growth. One way to do this is through reading books that empower and inspire. In this list, we've compiled a selection of books specifically written for the New Black Woman, covering wellness, career, relationships, and more. Whether you seek guidance, inspiration, or entertainment, these books are a great place to start.

- *The 1619 Project: A New Origin Story,* by Nikole Hannah-Jones

- *Be Unapologetically You,* by Adeline Bird

- *(The) Body Is Not an Apology, Second Edition: The Power of Radical Self-Love,* by Sonia Renee Taylor

- *Birthing Justice: Black Women, Pregnancy, and Childbirth,* edited by Julia Chinyere Oparah and Alicia D. Bonaparte

- *Caste: The Origins of Our Discontents,* by Isabel Wilkerson

- *Get Good With Money: Ten Simple Steps to Becoming Financially Whole,* by Tiffany Aliche

- *I'm Not Yelling: A Black Woman's Guide to Navigating the Workplace,* by Elizabeth Leiba

- *I'm Telling the Truth, But I'm Lying: Essays,* by Bassey Ikpi

- *Killing the Black Body,* by Dorothy Roberts

- *Own Your Glow: A Soulful Guide to Luminous Living and Crowning the Queen Within,* by Latham Thomas

- *Pleasure Activism: The Politics of Feeling Good*, by adrienne maree brown

- *Rest is Resistance: A Manifesto*, by Tricia Hersey, founder of The Nap Ministry

- *Right Within: How to Heal from Racial Trauma at Work*, by Minda Harts

- *The How: Notes on the Great Work of Meeting Yourself*, by Yrsa Daley-Ward

- *(The) Sacred Bombshell Handbook of Self-Love: The 11 Secrets of Feminine Power*, by Abiola Abrams

- *Self-Care for Black Women: 150 Ways to Radically Accept & Prioritize Your Mind, Body & Soul*, by Oludara Adeeyo

- *Set Boundaries, Find Peace: A Guide to Reclaiming Yourself*, by Nedra Glover Tawwab

- *Thick and Other Essays*, by Tressie McMillan Cottom

- *The Strong Black Woman: How a Myth Endangers the Physical and Mental Health of Black Women*, by Marita Golden

- *Unapologetic: A Black, Queer, And Feminist Mandate for Radical Movements,* by Charlene A. Carruthers

- *(The) Unapologetic Guide to Black Mental Health: Navigate an Unequal System, Learn Tools for Emotional Wellness, and Get the Help You Deserve,* by Rheeda Walker

- *Well-Read Black Girl: Finding Our Stories, Discovering Ourselves,* edited by Glory Edim

- *What Happened to You?: Conversations on Trauma, Resilience, and Healing,* by Oprah Winfrey, Bruce D. Perry, et al.

- *(The) Year of Yes: How to Dance It Out, Stand In the Sun and Be Your Own Person,* by Shonda Rhimes

- *You Are Your Best Thing: Vulnerability, Shame Resilience, and the Black Experience,* edited by Tarana Burke and Brené Brown

- *Your Next Level Life,* by Karen Arrington

MORE BOOKS FOR THE NEW BLACK WOMAN

In addition to the previous list, here are more books that can inspire and empower the New Black Woman. These books offer valuable insight. Whether you're looking for motivation, guidance, or a good read, these books are worth adding to your reading list.

- *Ain't I a Woman: Black Women and Feminism*, **by bell hooks:** seminal wits, wisdom, and perspectives on various aspects of Black womanhood, from memoirs and essay collections to self-help and business guidebook on the intersection of race, gender, and class in the feminist movement.

- *All About Love: New Visions*, **by bell hooks:** a deeply insightful exploration of the nature of love and how it can transform individuals and society.

- *(The) Autobiography of My Mother,* **by Jamaica Kincaid:** a novel that explores themes of family, identity, and colonialism in the Caribbean.

- *This Bridge Called My Back: Writings by Radical Women of Color,* **edited by Cherríe Moraga and Gloria Anzaldúa:** a groundbreaking anthology of essays, poetry, and fiction by women of color.

- *Hood Feminism,* **by Mikki Kendall:** a powerful exploration of how mainstream feminism often fails to address the specific issues women of color face.

- *Sister Outsider,* **by Audre Lorde:** a collection of essays and speeches by the influential poet and activist.

- *Sister Citizen: Shame, Stereotypes, and Black Women in America,* **by Melissa Harris-Perry:** a robust analysis of how Black women are often stereotyped and marginalized in American society.

- *(The) Source of Self-Regard,* **by Toni Morrison:** a collection of essays and speeches by the acclaimed author, covering topics such as race, literature, and society.

YOUR SOCIAL IMPACT

Giving back and mentoring the next generation are important ways to help uplift and empower Black women, who often face unique challenges and obstacles. Fortunately, many organizations and programs provide opportunities for Black women to give back and mentor others through education, career development, or personal growth. By sharing their skills, experiences, and wisdom, Black women can help shape the future and create a more equitable and just society. Here are various ways Black women can give back and mentor the next generation of New Black Women.

◊   Volunteer with Black Girls Rock! or similar organizations that empower Black girls and women. Some of these organizations include Black Girls Mentor Program, Black Girls Code, Girls Who Code, Sisters Code, Black Girls Golf, Black Girls Run, Black Girls Do Bike, National Black Women's Justice Institute, Black Women's Health Imperative, and The Brown Girls Guide to Politics. These organizations offer a range of programs and services, from mentorship and leadership development to

STEM education and physical fitness. By volunteering with these organizations, Black women can positively impact the lives of the next generation of Black girls and women.

◊ Mentor young Black girls through programs such as:

- **Girls Inc.:** a national organization that provides mentorship and educational programs to girls from underserved communities.

- **Big Brothers Big Sisters:** a mentoring program that pairs girls with adult women mentors to provide guidance and support.

- **Black Girls Code:** a program that teaches computer programming and technology skills to girls from underrepresented communities.

◊ Support Black-owned businesses and entrepreneurs to help build economic empowerment within the community. Here are some examples of Black-owned businesses and entrepreneurs to support:

- **The Honey Pot Company:** a plant-based feminine care company founded by Beatrice Dixon

- **BLK & Bold:** a specialty coffee and tea company that donates a portion of its profits to youth programming and workforce development initiatives

- **The Lip Bar:** a vegan and cruelty-free cosmetics company founded by Melissa Butler

- **CURLS:** a natural hair care brand founded by Mahisha Dellinger

- **McBride Sisters Collection:** a wine company established by sisters Robin and Andréa McBride

- *Taji* **Magazine:** a print and digital publication celebrating and uplifting Black culture

- **Me & the Bees Lemonade:** a lemonade company started by twelve-year-old Mikaila Ulmer

- **Pat McGrath Labs:** a luxury beauty brand founded by makeup artist Pat McGrath

- **The Crayon Case:** a makeup company founded by Raynell Steward, also known as "Supa Cent"
- **Uncle Nearest Premium Whiskey:** a whiskey company named after Nearest Green, a Black man who taught Jack Daniel how to distill whiskey

◊ Donate time or resources to organizations that promote education and career development for Black women, such as the Black Women's Career Network, which provides a supportive community, resources, and events to help Black women build their skills, network, and leadership abilities. The organization offers a range of programs, including mentorship, career coaching, job postings, and networking events, to help Black women succeed in various industries and levels of leadership. The Black Women's Career Network also partners with companies and organizations to promote workplace diversity, equity, and inclusion.

◊ Advocate for policies and legislation that promote equality and justice for Black women and girls. This can involve various actions such as:

- Contacting elected officials and advocating for policies and laws that address issues such as pay equity, access to healthcare, and criminal justice reform.

- Educating oneself and others about issues affecting Black women and girls, including systemic racism, sexism, and discrimination.

- Participating in protests, rallies, and other forms of activism to draw attention to issues affecting Black women and girls and demand change.

- Supporting organizations that advocate for policies and laws that promote equality and justice for Black women and girls, such as the National Black Women's Justice Institute or the Black Women's Health Imperative.

- Using social media and other platforms to raise awareness and advocate for issues affecting Black women and girls.

◊ Participate in community service projects that support Black women and families. You can:

- Volunteer at a local food bank or soup kitchen that serves predominantly Black communities.

- Participate in a community garden project that grows fresh produce for families in need.

- Help to build or repair homes for low-income families in Black communities through organizations like Habitat for Humanity.

- Volunteer at a local after-school or mentoring program serving Black girls.

- Organize a neighborhood clean-up or beautification project in a predominantly Black area.

- Support local organizations that provide resources and services to Black women and families, such as domestic violence shelters or job training programs.

- Host a book drive or collect school supplies for students in under-resourced Black communities.

- Participate in initiatives to increase voter registration and voter turnout in Black communities, such as voter education drives or rides to the polls.

- Help to organize or participate in community events that celebrate and uplift Black culture, such as Black History Month events or Juneteenth celebrations.

- Volunteer at a community health clinic that provides low-cost or free healthcare services to Black women and families.

◊ Share knowledge and expertise with young Black women through speaking engagements or workshops. Here are some examples:

- Volunteer to speak at a local school or community center about your career or personal experiences.

- Join a mentorship program that matches you with young Black women interested in your field.

- Offer to host a workshop or seminar on a topic you know about, such as financial literacy or entrepreneurship.

- Attend conferences or events that cater to Black women and offer to speak on a panel or lead a workshop.

- Collaborate with local organizations or groups serving Black women and offer training or guidance on a specific topic.

◇ Other ways to give back:

- Start a scholarship fund or contribute to existing ones that support Black women pursuing higher education.

- Sponsor a Black girl to attend a summer camp or program that aligns with her interests and talents.

- Volunteer as a coach or mentor for sports teams or extracurricular programs that serve Black girls.

- Support Black girls' involvement in STEM fields through organizations like Black Girls Code.

- Donate to organizations that provide resources for Black women and girls affected by domestic violence or sexual assault.

- Join a mentorship program or group that connects Black women with peers or mentors who can offer guidance and support.

- Attend conferences or events focusing on issues affecting Black women and share insights and knowledge gained.

- Host a book club or discussion group focused on literature and media created by Black women.

- Provide internships or job shadowing opportunities to young Black women interested in your field or industry.

- Volunteer as a tutor or mentor for Black girls struggling academically or socially.

- Offer pro bono or reduced-rate services to Black women and organizations serving Black communities.

- Serve on the board of directors or advisory committee for organizations that promote the advancement of Black women and girls.
- Advocate for representation and visibility of Black women in media and popular culture.

✦ ✦ ✦

As Black women, we face unique challenges and experiences that can impact our mental, emotional, and physical well-being. However, this guide is a testament to the resilience and strength of our community. Through the stories and insights shared in these pages, we hope to inspire and empower you to prioritize your self-care, set boundaries, and cultivate a positive mindset.

Remember, self-care is not selfish, and it is an essential practice that allows us to show up fully in all areas of our lives, including our work, relationships, and community. By caring for ourselves, we are better equipped to support others and create positive change in the world.

We hope this resource guide is a valuable tool for you on your journey to self-discovery, healing, and growth. May you continue to say yes to yourself, embrace silence, and prioritize your physical and mental health.

With love and support,
M.J. Fievre, author of *Badass Black Girl*

Marita Golden, author of *The Strong Black Woman*,
Saving Our Sons, and *The New Black Woman*

About the
Author

Marita Golden is a veteran teacher of writing and an acclaimed award-winning author of over twenty works of fiction, nonfiction, and anthologies. As a teacher of writing, she has served as a member of the faculties of the MFA Graduate Creative Writing Programs at George Mason University and Virginia Commonwealth University and in the MA Creative Writing Program at Johns Hopkins University. As a literary consultant, she offers writing workshops, coaching, and manuscript evaluation services.

Books by Marita Golden include the novels *The Wide Circumference of Love*, *After*, and *The Edge of Heaven*, the memoirs *Migrations of the Heart*, *Saving Our Sons*, and *Don't Play in the Sun: One Woman's Journey Through the Color Complex*, and the anthology *Us Against Alzheimer's: Stories of Family Love and Faith*. She is the recipient of many awards, including the Writers for Writers Award presented by Barnes & Noble and Poets and Writers, an award from the Authors Guild, and the Fiction Award for her novel *After* from the Black Caucus of the American Library Association. As a literary activist, Marita cofounded and serves as President Emerita of the Zora Neale Hurston/Richard Wright Foundation.

Mango Publishing, established in 2014, publishes an eclectic list of books by diverse authors—both new and established voices—on topics ranging from business, personal growth, women's empowerment, LGBTQ+ studies, health, and spirituality to history, popular culture, time management, decluttering, lifestyle, mental wellness, aging, and sustainable living. We were named 2019 *and* 2020's #1 fastest-growing independent publisher by *Publishers Weekly*. Our success is driven by our main goal, which is to publish high-quality books that will entertain readers as well as make a positive difference in their lives.

Our readers are our most important resource; we value your input, suggestions, and ideas. We'd love to hear from you—after all, we are publishing books for you!

Please stay in touch with us and follow us at:

Facebook: Mango Publishing

Twitter: @MangoPublishing

Instagram: @MangoPublishing

LinkedIn: Mango Publishing

Pinterest: Mango Publishing

Newsletter: mangopublishinggroup.com/newsletter

Join us on Mango's journey to reinvent publishing, one book at a time.